BLOGGING WEALTH SECRETS EXPOSED

Fred B. Norman

Blogging Wealth Secrets Exposed

Everything You Need to Make Money with Blogs

By Fred B. Norman

ISBN: 9798685156525

You will also like other best-selling eBooks in the category Internet Marketing from http://moneum.com.

 Web Magic Profits

This is our most popular package. This eBook tells everything you need to start generating incredible amounts of money in a web-based business. In this eBook you will learn important skills such as:

- Becoming an affiliate seller.

- Generating traffic.

- Creating websites that sell.

- Managing lists.

- And much more…

Product description: 112 pages, PDF format, with an Appendix, $29 (available now).

 The Affiliate Solution

Learn how to start a business without creating your own products! Promote some of the large number of the physical or digital products available in the Internet. In this information-packed eBook, your will learn:

- How to start as an affiliate.
- The importance of working in a niche.
- How to drive visitors to your campaigns.
- Using Google and Bing to display targeted ads.
- Using you email list to sell more.
- And much more…

Product description: 88 pages, PDF format, with an Appendix, $29

Legal Notice

While all attempts have been made to verify the information in this publication, neither the Author nor Publisher assumes any responsibility for errors, omissions, or contrary interpretations of the subject matter herein.

This publication is not intended as a source of legal or accounting advice. The publisher wants to stress that the information contained herein may be subject to varying state/local laws or regulations. All users are advised to retain competent legal counsel to determine what state and/or local laws or regulation may apply to the user's particular business.

The Purchaser or Reader of this publication assumes responsibility for the use of these materials and information. Adherence to all applicable laws and regulations, federal, state and local governing professional licensing, business practices, advertising and all other aspects of doing business in the United States or any other jurisdiction is the sole responsibility of the Purchaser or Reader.

The Author and Publisher assume no responsibility or liability, whatsoever on the behalf of the Purchaser or Reader of these materials.

Any perceived slights of people or organization are unintentional.

FOREWORD

Welcome to Blogging Success Secrets Exposed! This is a hands-on, no secrets-left-unrevealed guide to making money with blogs. If you are a beginning blog writer, who wants to turn your passion into a source of income, this is the right eBook for you. If you are an experienced blogger with a consolidated audience, this eBook will also give you many ideas to increase your profits.

We will explore together the big opportunities for money generation using blogs as your main tool. You will see how can you go from a beginner, without any experience in the area of blogging or internet business, and still make some money – or even a lot of money, if you so decide.

If you are an experienced blogger, this book will also have a lot of strategies for you too. Many bloggers are experts in generating content, but frequently they have little knowledge of how to use that content to produce cash. This untapped opportunity is available to you, and you can make much more money from your efforts than you ever felt possible.

Audience

Even expert bloggers will find a thing or two in this eBook that they can use right now and make more money! There are certainly many bloggers that are more experienced than I am, but by doing this eBook I have used not only my own experience but also the knowledge of many others that have created winning money-making strategies. This is the reason why I think anyone can benefit from the lessons contained in this short eBook.

If you have some money generating idea that is making your blog more profitable, please drop me a line. I would be very interested to discuss it and learn from you. Many of my readers have provided me with new insights about money generation using blogs --- and I will be happy to improve this eBook with whatever new strategies you want to share with our community. Just drop me a message at webmaster@showmeyourblog.com.

I also urge you to get more of our weekly tips for internet business. You just need to sign up for our newsletter at http://moneum.com.

INTRODUCTION

Blogging is a fantastic new way to publish information. As bloggers become more prominent in the media and the Internet, we have watched and learned about several success stories of common people that have made it big on the web.

People that started with a simple, small web site, with just some idea of what information they would like to share with the world. They started to create their web site in their spare time, with little or no outside help. However, by their own perseverance and will power, some people conquered a big slice of the attention from web readers everywhere.

The same people went on to conquer a space in the Internet by regularly pushing articles that captivated readers and gradually increased their online presence.

But, is this kind of success something that you can also achieve? Or it is just a temporary frenzy fed by the media, and that will stop as quickly as it started? This is the question that I would like to discuss with you initially. As it turns out, the answer to both questions above is yes, and no.

MAKING MONEY WITH YOUR IDEAS

Most people would like to have a shot at start making money with their personal abilities. People that know how to perform a craft, play an instrument, or run a business, or any other valuable skill in society, and would like to create some personal income from this knowledge.

Well, blogging might be just the opportunity you waited for. With blogging technology, which has been perfected in the last few years, you can create a viable business that converts your knowledge and personality into something that could become useful to thousands of people.

Blogs allow common folks like you and me to reach out to anyone in the world with a message. It doesn't really matter the particular topic: if you want to talk about a professional trend, or just about your latest craft, blogs can be the right platform to deliver your message.

To create a blog and increase your readership quickly, you just need to follow a few quick steps:

- Decide on what kind of information you want to share!

- Use your current knowledge of anything useful to write blog posts.

- Create a blog in a free website or get your own domain for better visibility.

- Post your articles to the recently created website that you control.

- Add monetization strategies, like short advertisements, AdSense, affiliate links, etc.

- Receive the money generated like this each month and deposit it in your bank account!

This is a simple system, but we will discuss each of these steps in the following chapters, so that you can have a clear picture of how the whole process works.

Spreading Your Message

You need to realize that it has never been easier to expose your ideas to a large audience, like nowadays. The print revolution (initiated by Gutenberg in Germany) made it possible to quickly duplicate books and other published material.

However, because of the costs involved, becoming a published author was still a difficult proposition, unless you had easy access to the printing services. Until recently you needed to find a literary agent or a publisher to print your book. In the case of magazines, you had to convince an editor that you had a great idea for an article.

Nowadays, in the Internet era, anyone with access to a personal computer (which can even be a public computer from a library, or Internet cafe, for example) can become an electronically published author.

And blogs are exactly the easiest way to make this happen on the web. No fees, no limitations of availability, you just to create a new post and save it in your blog.

But this simple invention called blog has not only revolutionized communication, but also marketing and business. It is now possible to create a blog on any business area and start making money from your knowledge!

This eBook will teach you how to do this. You may be starting from scratch, without any previous knowledge. Or you may already have some of this experience, and even have started your own blog, it doesn't matter.

Whatever your situation, I want to provide all information on how to make money from your blog. And you can use the results of my research to generate huge profits.

With a blog, you can create a big business making seven figures, or even more. Or you may use your blog to be just a small side-business, that generate good profits but that doesn't take much of your time. Whatever your goals, this eBook will provide you with tools and techniques to achieve it.

We hope you will not only read and learn this information, but also apply it to your own blog. If you apply even a small fraction of the techniques that I recommend in this eBook, I guarantee that you will achieve results.

WHY CREATING A BLOG?

The first question we would like to answer is what exactly a blog is, and why having one would make you so successful.

In general terms, a blog is a web site that uses software to separate content into small parts, called posts. Posts are generally ordered chronologically, so that users can see what is new.

The central concept in blogs, then, is that of fresh, new content. Users want to visit a blog that has the following elements:

•	Good content: the first requirement for writing a blog is having something to say. People spend time on the internet, and they are always looking for something new to learn about. If you have good information, you will attract those readers to your blog. However, boring and useless content will not endear with readers… No one will try to go back to a website that is disorganized and useless.

•	Articles focused on a topic that you enjoy: successful blogs are focused on a particular topic. They bring in people that are interested in the subject because they know there will be useful information. If you cannot determine a particular topic for your blog, then it will become very hard to achieve success in the long run.

•	Updated frequently: the other important characteristic of blogs is that they are frequently updated. This is important, because the more updates, the more people will have a reason to check back frequently on your blog. Frequent updates mean more opportunities to interact with readers.

AVOIDING MISTAKES

Here is a list of mistakes you should avoid when creating a new blog:

• Not updating frequently (at least once per week): blogs are different from other websites in which they need to be updated frequently. You don't need to post every single day, although some blogs are updated daily (and some even more than twice a day). However, you need to update frequently, at least once a week, to make your blog memorable. Less than that and your readers will find something else to read and stop following you.

• Writing long, boring posts: There is no problem in writing some long posts to use as promotional topics in your website. However, people are better at reading small amounts of text in the computer screen. If every post in your blog is a long essay, most people will think they don't have the time to follow you. Be concise and your readers will thank you!

• Writing predictable posts: lack of imagination is a terrible problem when you're doing any kind of writing. Avoid this by doing research into new topics you would like to write about. This usually shouldn't take too much time, and there are clear rewards.

• Going off topic: this is a pretty big problem for many writers. You have a blog on the topic "pajamas", and suddenly you start writing topics about the construction in your house! While there is no problem in talking a little about yourself, don't think that people will visit your blog just because of your personal life – unless you happen to be a very interesting person, such as an athlete, a top model, singer, or actress.

•	Not displaying your personality: even though you should attain yourself to your topic, it is also important to show that you have a personality. Everybody enjoys knowing that they're in contact with a real person. So, try to impress your personality, and it will make your readers more interested in what you're writing about, whatever the topic is.

•	Apathy: write posts where you show your excitement by the topic you're discussing. Excitement is contagious, and people will get more interested in what you have to say as a result. On the other hand, if you write with apathy and lack of enthusiasm, your readers won't have any interest in what you're saying.

SETTING UP A BLOG

I know that by now most people are familiar with what blogs are how they work. The general media has done a great job in the last few years in publicizing blogs and even in giving prominence to some bloggers, who have in a sense become celebrities in their particular fields.

However, most people still have little experience with the process of setting up you own blog. Even if you have done it before, it is still useful to have a reference work on how to do this. So, if you are experienced, feel free to skip this section and you can refer back to it when and if you need to create a new blog.

BLOG HOSTING

To create a new blog, the first decision you need to take is where to host it. There is a huge number of options these days, therefore you should be aware of how they are different and what are the advantages or disadvantages for someone that wants to make money from a blog.

These are some of he of different types of hosting available for blogs:

- Free hosting
- Cheap, small size web hosting
- Reseller webhosting
- Cloud based hosting
- Dedicated hosting

I will go through these options, so that you can find the one that best corresponds to your needs.

FREE HOSTING

If you're just starting a new blog and want to have a glimpse of how blogging works, you can just start a blog on free hosting websites. While there are tons of options for how to create a free blog, two of them are leaders in this space: Google blogger and wordpress.

Blogger is the blog platform maintained by Google. Having the support of a giant corporation is, without question, a plus of Blogger's offering. Blogger has been for many years the number one option for people looking for a free space to setup their blog.

If you already have a google account, creating a blogger-based blog is incredibly easy. You just need to login to http://blogger.com and enter some basic information, such as the name of the blog and a its sub-title. Then, you can select the look of your new blog from a large number of free templates.

Once you've setup the blog, the site offers a very intuitive composer that you can use to create new posts.

The second great option for free blogging is using WordPress. The WordPress web site allows you to easily create personal blogs. These blogs can then be managed using the same interface of the self-hosted WordPress software.

The biggest advantage of WordPress is the incredible number of plugins that have been developed for the platform. WordPress also gives you the possibility of migrating your account to paid services or to a self-hosted solution using the same software platform.

SHARED WEB HOSTING

Another option you have to host your blog is to pay for a cheap shared web hosting service. Some of these services cost around $5 a month, and some cost even less if you get a promotional deal. With this kind of hosting you can use your own domain (which is sometimes included in a package).

The advantage of such web hosting options is that for a small price they give you the ability to select the best software for you blog. In this way, you don't need to depend on software done by large companies.

Another important advantage is that you have complete control of the content of the blog: the data is all stored in servers that you control, instead of being stores by a company such as Google.

RESELLER WEB HOSTING

Some hosting companies offer deal for reseller web hosting. What this means is that you can have several domains served by the same account. This is a great advantage if you want to maintain more than one blog.

With a reseller web hosting you're free to create different websites in the same account. Thus, you can expand your business in an easier way, by avoiding the creation of a new hosting account for each different website.

CLOUD BASED HOSTING

Many hosting companies are nowadays migrating to a cloud-based hosting strategy. This means that hosted websites are stored in the cloud, not in a physical server owned by the hosting company.

Cloud based hosting can help in reducing costs when you need more than a single machine. This is ideal when your blog-based business is growing and more than one machine becomes necessary to handle the visitors. With cloud-based hosting, it becomes much easier and cost effective to support multiple machines.

DEDICATED HOSTING

A dedicated host is one in which a physical machine is dedicated to your website. This is a more expensive service, but it also gives you the guarantee that a machine is used exclusively by your blog (unlike shared hosting and reseller web hosting).

Dedicated web hosts are recommended when you have a blog with a large number of visitors. In this case, you want machines that are dedicated to your website, avoid annoying delays and other issues that might occur when you're using shared machines.

While dedicated hosting is worthy service when needed, as a starting blogger you probably don't need to worry about this. Using a less expensive service at the beginning is advisable, especially because you can upgrade your hosting account as necessary (hosting companies will gladly do this free work for you, as it means that you're upgrading to a more expensive option).

CREATING A BLOG IN A PAID HOST

In any of these paid options you will have dedicated software to create your new blog. Most hosting companies will point you to some interface that can be used to quickly create a new blog on your own domain. In most cases, the software gives the option of installing and using WordPress.

I highly recommend using WordPress as your blogging software. First of all, it is very widely used. This means that you will easily find people with technical knowledge to help you customize the blog according to your needs.

The other advantage of using WordPress is that it provides a large number of free customizations, in the form of plugins and templates. Plugins give additional features that are not found on the basic WordPress installation. Templates provide free (or sometimes paid) web designs for your blog. You can select from literally thousands of available options, which can help you customize your blog in practically any aspect.

GETTING FREQUENT VISITORS

When we start a blog, there are many topics that pop up to our mind as possible subjects. Then we write the first posts and these will attract a considerable number of people, most of them comprised of friends and acquaintances.

However, after a few days and weeks this kind of readership starts to dim down, as a few of them have no real interest in visiting your blog frequently.

This is when you need to start creating a loyal readership for your blog. You cannot just depend on the person who visits you blog occasionally. This in important traffic, but even better is the kind of reader that checks your blog frequently: every week, or even every day, depending on your writing schedule.

In order to conquer this kind of readership, you need to apply some tactics that will make them more inclined to check your posts with regularity. And as a result, automatically increase your income from the blog.

KEEPING A SCHEDULE

The number one idea to increase the number and frequency of your visitors is to write constantly. This is easily overlooked because it takes so much discipline to write constantly (even if it is just a few paragraphs). However, people do consider this when they decide what web sites or blogs to visit.

Think about this for a second. How excited would you be if you visited a blog regularly, let's say every week, and found out that the same post from two months ago was still at the front page? Not very excited, right?

The same goes for your readers. Just because you have a fancy blog theme, with lots of links and pictures of yourself, it doesn't mean that visitors will want to come back day after day.

What they want is to read your content, nothing more.

In order to keep them coming back, you need to provide information that is reliable, and timely. You have to create some kind of hook that will turn them from sporadic visitors into regulars.

Writing regularly will ensure that visitors get something back every time they stop by. It becomes a feedback loop. It is instant rewarding, the kind of experience that everyone likes to have.

Creating constancy and consistency in your writing schedule may seem complicated at first, especially if you're just starting, but it becomes really easy after you apply a few tips.

CONSIDER READER PREFERENCES

First, try to gauge from your blog stats what topics people enjoy the most. Are they hooked into your how-to articles on growing tulips? Or your recipes for baked potato?

Once you understand what makes them tick, just repeat it. Yes, just give them what they are looking for! Keep also watching the stats and trying to understand if this strategy is really working or not. Then change the topic if necessary.

By the way, you need to understand that some readers may not like you repeating some kinds of posts. This is natural, because not everyone likes the same things. A small part of your readers may not enjoy baked potato recipes at all.

However, remember that you're writing for the whole audience, not for a minority. Moreover, after a while they will also get used to your topics, and the few that don't will ultimately leave your blog anyway. You should consider your larger comunity of readers and do what is best for them.

CREATE AN IDEA BACKLOG

Another thing that will help keep your consistency is creating a backlog of ideas for posts. In my experience, the process of writing a post is simple. It doesn't take more than a few minutes to put a few paragraphs together.

However, it takes some time to figure out about what to write. This may delay your process and result in sub-par posts that will not be enjoyed by visitors.

To avoid this, always create a backlog of ideas that you would like to talk about. Whenever you have an idea that could become a blog post, just write it down: a few words are enough.

When the time comes, instead of thinking about a new topic, just take one from your backlog, and write a quick post. It is easy, and it takes just a few minutes.

The idea of keeping a backlog is important because you will start to collect ideas from everyone, even from readers themselves.

For example, comments to your posts will sometimes give suggestions for what to write next. Use these ideas: the commenter will even be proud of seeing his or her ideas developed as a post in your blog. Especially if you give the due credit.

Another source of ideas for a backlog is the list of Google searches that hit your site. You can get this information from any analytics package – and by the way, the easiest one is Google analytics itself.

These analytics packages show the list of keywords that people were searching when they reached your blog through Google. So, you can make the life of web searchers easier, and make sure that your blog is relevant for that kind of question.

Suppose for example, that you have a blog about flowers, and you see a blog search for a specific product in that industry. This is an excellent sign that you can write a blog post talking about how to use that product: this is something that your readers are already looking for.

This kind of search listing is very important, because some of the topics will appear very frequently. If you see five or more searches of the same kind for a specific keyword, this means that there is a lot of readers interested in that topic.

When that happens, just use the opportunity and optimize your pages for that subject. Or create a separate post that is specific to that particular query, and you will probably see your traffic increase for that page.

Even more important, the more visitors you have coming through Google and similar web sites, the more keywords you have at your disposal. They will serve as suggestions for what posts you can write. You can view than as clues for what users want, so you can continue to produce regular content.

RESERVE TIME IN YOUR SCHEDULE

Still, another idea for adding regularity to your posts is to set up specific time slots when you expect to create new content. A problem that many new blog writers have is assigning no particular time for writing the blog.

Remember, although a blog is supposed to be easy to write, it doesn't mean it is completely effortless. You have to spend some time to flesh out ideas, answer comments, check for new topics, and for the writing itself.

The ideal is to have a separate block of time every few days. In this way, you can keep up with how your blog is going, without a sense of overwhelming that is so common when we don't have specific goals.

For example, you can create a schedule where you take Tuesdays and Thursdays to write posts, and Fridays to create new ideas and clean up the blog.

Having such a schedule means that you will be more in control of the process, without having to take time from other activities that will be constantly going on.

Also, it creates a better sense of control from the part of your readers. Many of them will understand that you generally write new posts on Tuesdays and Thursdays, and will be eager to read them as the time comes. This is a very good way to suggest a regular schedule to your readers, and they will also be glad you are following a predictable pattern.

GETTING IDEAS
FOR POSTS

In the mind of young entrepreneurs, one of the biggest hurdles to create a successful blog is having enough content to regularly add to the blog.

This fear, that in some ways is similar to the fear of public speaking, is something that can be easily dealt with. Creating content for any blog is not a difficult proposition.

First of all, if you are starting a blog in the way I suggested, it will be in a topic that you know about well. The test to know if you are knowledgeable about an area is the following: can you talk something about it without doing prior research?

If your answer is yes, then you already have what takes to become a blogger in the subject. Your blog is not supposed to provide authoritative information on a new subject. For this purpose, there are books, dissertations, and trade journals.

A blog is mostly dedicated to light commentary on issues that pertain to a particular field. For this to work, you just need to be perceived as an insider, someone that knows what is going on in an area.

In no way you need to create blog entries that will improve on the knowledge of the area you are considering, although there is nothing wrong with doing this...

For an example, suppose you want to create a blog about smart phones. To do this, you don't need to be a cell phone engineer: although that is could be valuable, it is not necessary.

You should be capable, however, to talk competently about what is going on in the cell phone industry nowadays: what new devices are coming this year, how good they are, what recommendations you have, etc.

THINK AS A USER, NOT AS A SPECIALIST

This shows another aspect of blogging that is important for entrepreneurs. If you want to make money with a blog, it is better if you put yourself in the shoes of a consumer than of a specialist.

The universe of people that use a product is much more interested in the perceptions of other users than in the technical aspects of the product. If you want a bigger readership for your blog, it pays to approach your area as an informed user.

In the given example, it is much more interesting to write as someone that buys cell phones and give recommendations and tips on its use. The other view, of a specialist in cell phones, is less useful because few people can identify with it.

USE A CONVERSATIONAL STYLE

Another tactic for creating good blog posts and attracting more readers is to avoid the mentality of formal writing, and instead adopting more of a conversational style.

The difference here is that official-style writing is more formal and elaborate. In this case, you are forced to use long words, and make sure that the organization of the document is formally correct.

In a conversation, however, we are much less interested in formalities, and more interested in keeping the flow of communication.

Successful bloggers create posts that sound more like a conversation than a formal discourse. Your readers will feel more engaged this way, because they will look at yourself more as a friend that is chatting about something familiar, rather than an impersonal source of information.

What would you like better: to look as person or a machine? I would much better prefer to be viewed as human.

FINDING A NICHE

If you want to be successful with blogging, you need to find a specific area that you want to write about. The issue is, unless you are already a famous person, nobody will be interested in visiting your blog if there is no clear benefit to him or her.

If, beyond that, you want to make a profit with your blog, you need to clearly identify a niche.

In market terms, a niche is a very specific area in which you can reach customers for a particular kind of service or product. There are as many niches as there are classes of products, and all are defined by things that people can buy.

For example, there are niche markets for beauty products, for computer gadgets, for fashion accessories, and many others. Only your imagination is the limit for the possible niches you can identify.

DO THINGS YOU ARE PASSIONATE ABOUT

A big mistake made by beginners is to try to make money by creating a blog in a field that they have no personal connection just a way to make money. This may seem smart at first, but it rarely works.

The problem is that creating and maintaining a blog takes some work, for long periods of time. If you have to work in an area that you don't know well and, more importantly, in a field that you don't care about, it is difficult to find the motivation to keep going.

Most people will simply start a project, and in a few days or weeks lose the interest in that project. Then, they will mark that as a failure and stop blogging altogether.

To avoid this kind of situation, it is better to make first a personal assessment of your desires and personal interests:

- Is this an area that I know well?

- Is this an area that I don't know very well but have a deep interest in learning?

- Can I integrate this field into other activities (either personal or professional) in my life?

- Can I spare sometime every few days to research and create new content (posts) related to this area?

If you can answer yes to at least two or more of these questions, then you could create a good blog in this particular area. Otherwise, the possible lack of interest may be an unfortunate reason for the failure of you project. Don't let this happen!

THERE MUST BE FINANCIAL INTEREST IN IT

Remember that to monetize your blog, you have to create content in an area that has some marketing activity. So, before you begin to create your blog, try to determine if the area you want to write about has already any marketing activity (the more the better).

Most people will visit and read blogs about diverse activities and experiences. However, to make a living on it, you also need readers that are interested in buying products. Without this kind of readers, it becomes very difficult to maintain your blog as a money-producing activity.

A good way to determine if a blog would be able to sustain itself is to use a keyword research tool to see what the competition is doing. If you go to Google website, you can search for Good Ads Planner, the free tool provided by Google to investigate words you want to use in an ad campaign.

The importance of using such tools in gauging competition and market opportunity resides in knowing that a segment of the market is interested in what you plan to offer. If many people are bidding for a specific keyword related to your niche, this means that many readers are buying based on clicks for these keywords.

Another possible way to determine the size the market for a keyword is to go directly to Google search. Type your topic, and see what kind of results you get. If you see lots of ads vying for your attention, this means that there is a ready market for your information product. As I said before, it is always easier to sell products in a well-established market than in a field that has no commerce at all.

Another advantage of this strategy is that you can see what kind of offers are being presented to people typing the same keywords. Therefore, you can easily use these ads as another source for your own research on which companies are offering products, and which products they're selling in the niche you've chosen.

COMBINE PASSION AND PROFITS

Once you've concluded your research, you're now in a position to determine the field that gives you the better chance of becoming successful as a blogger. Remember that you need to combine both factors described above: passion and profits.

Every person is different, and the needs of the market are also incredibly varied. This means that you can easily find something that you are deeply interested and that at the same time have great commercial value. Creating a blog in this intersection will give you optimal chances of becoming successful and at the same time profiting from what you enjoy!

HOW FREQUENTLY SHOULD YOU POST?

Another question frequently asked by newcomers to the blogging world is how frequently should they post new articles to their blog.

Everything we have seen up to now suggests that a higher posting frequently usually translates in more money and visibility for the blog.

However, there is a limit that you need to consider as useful, and depending on what this limit is, you will have a different kind of blog, that will appeal to a different segment.

So, lets first talk about the normal kind of business owner that we have in mind: someone that wants to create a viable business where the blog is one of the main promotional tools. The blog will be monetized using advertisement or by selling products, which can be from the same owner of the blog or affiliate products.

This is a true-and-tested strategy to create a blog that will generate enough income to maintain a profitable business.

If you this is what you're looking for, then I would say that posting at least once a week is the best way to go. Less than once a week may work against of you for several reasons:

•	Your readership is usually dependent on the number of posts, because posts are the main tool to attract readers. Having very few posts means that your readership base will increase very slowly, so it is probably not a profitable business.

• If you post less than once a week, you will frequently have stale posts in the front page. This means that readers will feel bored and unmotivated to access you blog again.

• You want to get readers used to your style. If you post infrequently, it makes it harder to develop this style and voice that would be another attractive aspect of your blog.

• It is also harder to sell advertisement in a blog that is not updated frequently. Most metrics in blog advertisement are based in number of accesses. This metric will be lower for blogs that have only a few posts.

Thus, you see that writing at least once a week is a good thing for your blog. Some people prefer to post twice a week, let's say, one at the beginning of the week and another towards the end.

The exact number of times you post is of course up to you, but I would suggest a maximum of one per day.

There are a few days when you might have a lot to say, and clearly there is nothing wrong with more than one post per day.

However, there are a few risks if you try to add more than one post per day, and you must be aware of them, before you think this is the solution for all your problems.

One of the risks is that you might run out of what to say. Yes, I know it is not so hard to write blog posts, but it sometimes happens. In fact, the web is littered with blogs where the authors have been so keen on filling the blog with posts, that it becomes completely out of topic.

When people out-post like this, the first thing that happens is that they transform a niche blog into a general-purpose blog. I see this all the time happening, for example, in technology.

A blogger decides to start a blog in a niche topic of technology, let's say a specific type of gadget or cell phone. Then, in order to make ends meet and get more advertisement, the blogger start loading the web site with all kinds of posts that are tangential to the topic.

The next thing you see is that the blog is now about everything technology. They will start to cover new things by Microsoft, Apple, and all other tech companies, usually will ill prepared blog posts.

When this happens, these guys are basically trying to compete with newspapers, magazines, and all other blogs. If they succeed, they will end up making a lousy return of investment for all that effort, exactly because there are already thousands of traditional vehicles for this type of news.

Another insidious problem with posting too much, is that it will bore your readers. Some of them will feel tired of following your blog, and after a few days will just say "enough". Many people like to read web sites, but they also need to work and do other productive things.

Then, other people will start to realize that you're not talking about your specific topic, but has become a general media blog. These people will also become unhappy with the lack of focus and leave your blog.

So, there are several reasons why blogging too much may not be the solution for your problems. Remember that you want to be viewed by your readers as someone that is different, and is a specialist in the topic you're talking about, not somebody trying to make a quick buck by selling advertisement on meaningless posts.

Still another issue that you need to worry about when blogging too frequently is burn out. I will talk about this in the next section.

Niche Blogs vs. News Blogs

Not understanding the difference between niche blogs and large-scale news websites may also lead to problems for the beginning blogger. In this case, burnout may become an issue, and it can make or break a business based on the blog model. This is again linked to the anxiety of producing too frequent posts that we discussed above.

So, I will discuss the issues with some types of blogging sites that I think are not useful for most single entrepreneurs, and why they are should be avoided. In fact, a number of web sites these days have become something more than a blog, which is quite distinct from what we are discussing on this eBook.

I am talking here about popular blogs that have in fact become independent news sources, similar to online newspapers, such as Engadget, Huffington Post, and others. While these websites have initially being labeled as blogs, they are something quite different.

While it is interesting that these sites have brought visibility to world of blogging, there are also some unfortunate aspects in they being labeled by some as "blogs". The unfortunate point is that this brings some unrealistic expectations to new bloggers, who may be convinced to try a model that may not be achievable.

Not everyone who starts a blog will be as successful as the creators of Engadget or Huffington Post. And that is all right! Creating a large website also doesn't guarantee profitability, which is always our plan for niche-oriented blogs.

The main issue here is that a web sites as Engadget have become something much bigger than a blog. While on the surface these web sites continue to have entries ordered chronologically, and still use similar software, such as wordpress or typepad, they have morphed into large scale operations that are out of reach for the individual, small business blogger.

On the contrary, most of these high-profile blogs are in fact news web sites posing as blogs – mostly for a marketing reason.

As we see, the real difference is that such web sites operate almost like a newspaper or on line magazine. They are staffed with hired or free-lance writers/reporters that cover a general area that is of interest to the larger media.

Just to clarify, here is another notable difference you can find in such large-scale news blogs: they are frequently not the product of a sole entrepreneur. Although they might have started as such, some high-profile news blogs are put together by a team of investors that want to get a high return on their investment.

As a consequence, some of these web sites have received millions of dollars in funding. A big example of this trend is The Huffington Post. By following this model, similar to many high-tech start-up companies, the entrepreneur loses large part of the control of the company, and is required to work for a board of investors, in order to return their money.

Even when the entrepreneur has a majority stake, he or she still need to put a lot of work to maintain investors satisfied – otherwise they can "pull the plug" on that investment and the founder will lose everything!

While this kind of high-stress environment might appeal to some entrepreneurs, it is definitely not the ideal environment for everyone.

BLOG MONETIZATION STRATEGIES

One of the best things of blogs is that they may pay well! You can create a web site that you can update only a few times a week, and people all over the world will be paying you to have access to it.

Wait, did I say paying? But aren't your readers accessing the blog free of charge? After all, information is free in the Internet, isn't it?

Well, while it is true that people can see your posts for free, this doesn't mean that they won't pay you in some way for your effort. In fact, if you attract loyal visitors to your web site, they will be paying in several ways as we will see next.

In this chapter, I will give you the tips you need to get your readers to pay in a way that is fun for them and for you. These techniques are the way you will use to monetize your blog, that is, to convert readership into money in your pocket.

DISPLAYING ADS

The basic strategy to convert your blog into a money generating machine is to display advertisements. And there are several ways to make this possible.

Web based ads came a long way in the last few years. In the beginning, these ads consisted almost exclusively of banners that you would display on the web site.

These banners could be entertaining, but they were also very unproductive. In the web, most people learned to disregards banner images, because it is so easy to do so.

A banner is the easiest thing to spot in a web page, and therefore it is really easy to turn it off when reading content.

Instead of banners, the next wave of web advertisement was based on text links. This is a much better way to engage readers because they are already interested in reading about your content. If they see a bunch of text ads, they will at least have the opportunity to read over, and eventually get interested if it is something that they relate to.

The biggest name of this kind of web advertisement is Google. Most of its money is generated by creating text links with advertisement that are added to any web page, including their search engine.

What makes text ads so powerful is that they can be truly related to what you're reading. For example, when discussing the latest digital camera that you bought on the weekend, the ads displayed on that content will be related to digital cameras.

This is much harder to do with pictures, since it is not easy for a computer to understand the match between a picture of a digital camera and the content of the web page.

Moreover, image ads take much more space than text-based ads. You can display lots of text ads in the same space that would be taken by a banner, for example.

For all these reasons, presenting text ads is probably the easiest to way to start monetizing your blog. You can select a few small areas initially, and use them to test the ads.

To start presenting text ads there are several options. The easiest one is the AdSense program by Google. The main reason is that they pay well compared to other programs. Also, they have a huge number of advertisers. This means that it is much easier to find some product that would be appropriate for the kind of subject you are writing about.

For example, if you write about the health care industry, you really want advertisement that is related to health issues. It would be a loss of time and money to present ads on furniture, for example. Your readers are expecting to get more of that topic, not of a different subject.

JOINING AN ADVERTISEMENT PROGRAM

If you are not yet a member of Google Ads, or a similar advertisement program, you should really start now. The process is really simple: you go to adsense.com, then enter some information about you such as name and address, and you will receive an identification code that can be used in your pages.

To display the ads, you need to past the code snippet provided in the AdSense site into one or more of your pages. The code simply loads the ads when a user enters the web page. This is done using Javascript, the common programming language used by all web browsers.

In order to display the right ads, Google needs some information about the space available in your page. Therefore, you need to choose between a set of predefined ad sizes.

The most common size is similar to a banner, and can be added to the top of the page. Other standard sizes include small and medium rectangles, that can be easily inserted in the middle or end of text blocks.

The use of these standard ad sizes makes it very easy to mix your content with Google ads. The more you are able to mix these ad blocks, the more frequently you will see customers clicking on them.

Notice that it is to your advantage to make sure that ad blocks are in a visible location, compared to where your standard blog content is located.

For example, lots of bloggers make the mistake of locating the Google ads in the opposite side from where the posts are. If you do this, there will be little chance that readers can see or read the copy of these ads. This results in poor conversion.

What improves conversion in just making sure that users will have an opportunity to read the ads as they glance through your original content.

A powerful method to do this is to have ads appearing in particular sections of the post. For example, the beginning of sections is a very attractive area, because that's how readers get a glimpse of what the post is about.

Therefore, adding small Google Ads blocks to the beginning of a section can increase its conversion dramatically.

Another area where you can add Google Ad blocks for great profit is the very end of posts. The reason is that the final words of a post is also a magnetic area. This happens simply because the final words bring a conclusion to your thoughts, and readers usually want to see the conclusion.

People love to hover around a post in order to see if it is important. One of the simple ways to do this is looking at the beginning and end of sections. The end of a post usually gives a very vivid description of the ideas that lead to the conclusion of your blog entry.

This is why readers are directed to that area. A sense of continuity also happens when you get to the end of a post. Have you noticed, for example, that it is hard to get to the end of a book chapter without going to the beginning of the next? It is the same thing with this technique.

Readers will be very interested in getting continuity from you writing, and they will automatically read what is right after your post. If you post a Google Adsense block there, you will get increased response.

This assumes, of course, that your article is of interest to you readers. The response to ads is proportional to the quality of your posts, and this is something that Google knows very well. That's why they are so keen on ranking good web sites according to how long people stay on that page, or how many links exist to your blog.

CREATING YOUR OWN PRODUCTS

Advertisement is a pretty easy way to create some fast income from your blog, and it is the first tactic used by people starting in this business field.

However, although advertisement is simple, it doesn't need to be the only, or even the first monetization strategy that you need to follow. Plenty of other opportunities exist, especially if you want to promote your own products on your blog.

If you already have a business and is creating a blog as a marketing strategy, then this is the ideal and most straightforward way to generate profits.

However, even if you have no other business other than the blog itself, it is still wise to consider creating and promoting your own products through the blog.

In that case, the kind of product you can create will depend directly on the topic of your blog. For example, my wife has a blog on manual crafts. For her it is really easy to create products that will be promoted through the blog. It is just a matter of creating a new craft, opening a new account in an auction site such as eBay, and listing the craft in her posts.

You probably can use a similar method in your blog. For example, a blog talking about cars may have listings of cars that you currently want to sell. Remember, if it is something that you're already doing, the overhead of selling the same product on the blog is very little.

A similar strategy that I will be talking about in more detail later is to sell somebody else's product. In its simplest form, you can go to a friend or another person that you know that has a product, then sell it in your blog and split the profits.

CREATING INFORMATION PRODUCTS

If you can find somebody else's information product to sell in your blog, you can generate profits in a very quick and straight-forward way.

Now, suppose that you are creating a blog in an area for which you don't have any product. You also can't even find somebody else that has a product to sell in that area. You may suppose that the situation is hopeless and just stop trying to sell something through your blog...

Well, maybe you shouldn't stop so quick. In fact, there is a kind of product that, while you might not have initially thought of, is pretty easy for you to create. And, in fact, you are already creating one.

What I am talking about is an information product. Information products are a category that includes most types of material that is published and sold in the world. It includes:

- eBooks
- Special Reports
- Audio books
- Manuals
- Video courses
- And much more...

TYPES OF INFORMATION PRODUCTS

eBooks:

The eBook is the type of information product you're reading right now! It is shorter than a normal book and more to the point, presenting exactly what your readers need to know about a specific topic. The same way I created this eBook from my research and experience with blog creation, you can also create your own eBook from your personal experience.

It may sound a little complicated at first, but the reality is that anyone with some practical knowledge is able to create an eBook. I explain how you can quickly create your own eBook, sometimes in less than one day, in another product: Magic Web Profits (check http://webmagicprofits.com for more information).

You can sell eBooks for a good profit if you market them on your blog. Prices vary, but you can charge from $20 to as much as $100, depending on how you package the information.

You might want to start charging a lower price to attract more customers. However, one thing you might consider is to have affiliates selling your product. If you want to do this, which I think you definitely should, then a pay of $20 per affiliate is quite common. Which means that you need to charge a price starting from $30, in order to have at least a $10 profit.

Special Reports:

A special report is a short document (from 5 to 20 pages) that explains your ideas about a very specific point that is of interest for your audience.

Special reports are even easier to write than an eBook. In a single day you can write one or more special reports and put them for sale on your page. People will want to access your special report if you cover a very particular and important topic.

You can sell them for as little as $10, or even for free if you want. The idea of special reports is that they can be used as a form of advertisement. You are also showing your readers the kind of useful information that you can provide. If readers like the report, in the future they will be more willing to buy an eBook.

Recorded material:

Nowadays it is easy to create an mp3 or video of your work, including online classes, speeches, or seminars. Depending on what activity you're doing, you can record it and sell it on your blog. For example, if you give a seminar on financial literacy you could video record it, then sell the recording on your web site.

If you have a Mac computer, this is even easier since there is a free software that comes with every Mac to edit video. Windows users can find similar software too, including Camtasia, which is frequently used to create video content.

If you create a complete information package including video recordings, eBook, and other resources, you can sell it for $100 or more, depending on the niche. I have even seen these packages being sold for more than $1000 and they are quick to sell if you have the right audience.

Imagine the profits you can make with these information products. Selling 10 copies of an eBook for $40 will bring you $400 per day. And the number of people interested in that product will only increase as you get more readers.

With some effort you can sell even 100 copies of an eBook and make up to $4000.

But remember that you can sell much more than a single eBook. You can create other eBooks and start doing the same thing. So, you don't need to sell 100 copies of a single product to make lots of money. You can sell a few copies of several products and achieve the same results.

And if you have at least one of these high value/high price products, you can even sell just one unit per day and make a living of it. It is just a matter of providing information that matters, at the right price point.

To see how different prices can help you, notice that some people may be initially interested only on a $5-dollar report. While this is not a big profit, it may be the beginning of a great relationship, where the customer can try more of your products as they like the information you have to offer.

Thus, someone that starts spending just a few dollars can end up buying hundreds or even thousands of dollars from you. It is a very profitable proposition that you can start by just putting your knowledge in a form that users can access!

WRITING YOUR OWN BOOK

Eventually, as you become successful as a producer of information products, you might want to go to the next step and have your own published (or self-published) book.

From the point of view of creating the content, writing a book is not very different from an eBook. You will follow more or less the same process.

However, the biggest difference is that you have to learn to interact with a separate industry: the book publishing industry, that has its own set of rules and standards.

So, although the creative process is similar, you have to define your goals in a more precise way when writing a book. For example, there are some questions you may need to answer before you write a single word of a Book.

First of all, is the book going to be published with a traditional publisher? If the answer is yes, then you need to define a few important things such as:

1.   Book agents: Are you going to use an agent to sell this book? Many traditional publishers require an agent in order to even consider new proposals. While you may try to find a publisher by yourself, it is just easier to use the services of someone who is specialized in this area.

2.   A proposal: Writing a good, attractive proposal is a key element to get a book contract signed. The book proposal is the tool used by publishers to decide if a book is worthy to be published or not.

3.   Negotiating an advance: Writing a book for an established publisher usually requires signing a contract. The contract defines an advance fee, that will cover your costs for writing the book.

4.   Details of the contract: There are several details in a book contract that you should check by yourself or find a lawyer that can help you. Among these items are the rights for electronic editions, foreign editions, and future derivative works (movies, audio books, etc.).

5.   Marketing: You will have to provide a lot of information on how to market your book and what would be the right audience. Depending on the kind of book, you will be required to appear on promotional events, such as radio shows, local or national news. In terms of marketing, there is no limit to how much work you may want to do for a book. It can range from nothing to a full-time job of book promotion.

The nice thing about writing a book is that the more you market, the more money you can potentially make on it. Since it is a well-established medium, you can use many more avenues than just the Internet.

As mentioned above, there are thousands of radio stations in this country that can be used as a vehicle to market a new book. All these marketing venues can be combined in order to generate publicity for you and your book.

There are many people that make a good living by promoting just a single book. Some of them became famous by doing so. For example, there is a guy who sells a book called "Free Money", which is basically a list of programs from the Government that provide money under certain conditions. He has made a full-time living just by selling this book on TV, radio, and other media.

Another person who became famous (or infamous) selling a book is Kevin Trudeau, who has published information books such as "Natural Cures They Don't Want You to Know About". He once mentioned that he had sold more than 30 million dollars from only one of his books. Do your calculations and you will have some idea of how much money he is making just selling information.

Clearly, these guys are working full time on this business, and they are consummate salesmen. However, you can also sell a lot of books on your own blog for your own niche. You should consider going this path if it is something that you find enjoyable.

SELF-PUBLISHING A BOOK

Self-publishing is another profitable revenue source you may want to pursue when creating a book to advertise in your blog. Self-publishing has become much more common these days, with the advent of web-based companies such as Lulu or CreateSpace (now part of Amazon). These companies can publish your new book in a matter of days, instead of months or years, as it happens with traditional publishers.

When you self-publish a book, there are a number of issues that you need to decide. For example:

•	How are you going to market the book? The number one question is the possible ways you can sell this book. We already know that you will want to use your blog, but is that enough to publicize your work? Maybe you should think of other venues to sell your book. For example, you can use seminars, local fairs, and other opportunities to sell additional copies.

•	How is the book going to be manufactured? Here there are several possibilities that you may want to investigate. The most popular services these days are Lulu and CreateSpace. Both allow you to set up an account for free, and create as many books as you can. The only thing you need to do is to order a physical copy for reviewing, before the book is made available for other buyers.

•	How to create the layout and cover? One issue that you need to handle when creating a self-published book is the artwork. While established companies already have a team of graphical designers to create a professional book cover and book layout, you need to do that by yourself. While this may look like a big problem, in fact there are several on line companies that will handle this work for a fee. Finally, if you don't want to spend any money, you can still do it yourself using common software such as Microsoft Word, for example.

Whatever the decision you make, writing and publishing a book is not as difficult as you can imagine. The ideas above barely scratched the number of possibilities when you use books to generate profits from your blog.

Another idea for book creation is just using your blog content. Remember that the content of your book can be anything from your past experience. A simple thing you can do, therefore, is just to expand the content of your blog posts into a longer version. Each of these can serve as a new chapter of your own book.

Remember that in the same way you can write a blog writing small posts every day, you can also write a whole book by creating a section per day. At the end of a few months you will have enough material to create a book on any topic.

Given the possibilities available to explore and the fact that your own blog already provides material that you can use, writing a book is, in my opinion, a relatively easy way to generate some extra income.

WRITING POWERFUL POSTS

One of the best ways to be noticed in the blog world is to write powerful posts that attract new viewers. To do this, you need to be able to create blog posts that are considered useful by a lot of people.

When this happens, you blog will explode in popularity and goes viral. A viral blog post is one that is recommended by everyone, until practically everybody in your niche visits it.

To create powerful, viral blog posts you need to research what are the main concerns and interests of your target group. If they are car enthusiasts, it must be something that relate to every car owner. In a blog about pets, you need to find something that will be amusing and useful to every pet owner.

Finding this type of topics maybe appear difficult sometimes, but once you have a little of experience reading and writing them, you will see that a pattern emerges.

To understand how this works, you should visit an aggregator site such as Reddit, for example. These web sites rank web posts according to votes cast by readers. Therefore, if you look at the items in the top position you will see the topics that appear most interesting to readers in general.

It may be that the topics at the top of Reddit are not interesting for your specific niche, but you can nonetheless learn a lot from them. Usually, one of the tricks you can use is to adapt a topic from one area to another. You would be surprised to see how frequently this works.

CHOOSE A TITLE FOR YOUR ARTICLE

Another trick that you will notice in these top posts is the importance of a catchy title. Most successful blog posts have in common a good title that attract readers.

To be successful, a title can have one of several features such as: invoking a strong emotion: hate, love, disgust, etc.; using anchor numbers; promising the revelation of secrets; or presenting research that is previously unknown to the readers.

For example, post titles that evoke emotions are very powerful because the attract the empathy of readers. For instance, "things that I hate about cell phones" is a good title because it attracts any user that had a problem with their mobile phones in the past.

Similarly, "reasons why I love my electronic reader" would be useful for people that don't have an electronic reader and want to know why people love them.

Other emotions such as disgust, disbelief, and surprise, for example, are excellent ways to highlight your title. It is much better to title your blog "Things that surprised me in my last trip" than just "my last trip". The later one doesn't convey any emotion to readers, so why should they spend time reading about it? On the other hand, a surprise is exciting for anyone, it certainly something that would be useful to read about.

Remember, if it a post title doesn't convey any emotion, it becomes a tough sell, unless it has some of the other elements we will mention. People are reading blogs mostly for amusement, and secondarily to learn something new. If you don't convey excitement on the title, there is little reason for users to read such a blog post.

It is just human nature that we prefer to relate to information that is given on emotional terms. In the same way you are much more inclined to watch a movie if there is action or romance, or whatever emotion you are more inclined to. Articles are not different, although they are using a different medium.

Using definite numbers is another trick that can dramatically increase your results. For example, readers love articles that provide "7 ways to increase your income", or the "top ten reasons why you need to buy stocks".

When you frame the topic into a definite quantity, it makes easier for readers to evaluate what you're offering. It you write "5 questions you want to answer", this is much more powerful than "questions you want to answer". People are attracted to what is easier to understand, and the version with a number is always easier to grasp.

You can also improve that by adding another dimension to the number; for example, you can use time to get an even greater sense of immediacy. So, using the post title above as example, we can improve it by saying "7 ways to increase your income in 2020". Now we are not only saying how many items we're offering, but also defining the time frame for the information. In other words, it is something urgent, that the reader should be aware as soon as possible.

Writing a killer headline may be easy if you pay attention to what the top magazines and web sites are doing. You will see these tricks repeated over and over again. Some people might believe that this happens only because writers are lazy and don't know better. The reality is that they do this because it works.

Another powerful way to create articles is to write a how-to. If you know how something is done and it is related to your blog, just write a how-to article: "how to plant a tree" or "how to save for your wedding". Even better would be "how to save for your wedding in 5 easy steps".

This kind of information can make your blog pretty popular, because it is providing not only commentary, but also reference information. Reference information is the kind of data that you want to review over and over again, when presented with a specific situation.

A reference article is also a powerful tool because it can be linked to by other people. Suppose someone is writing an article that talks about how to cultivate a garden. Instead of writing a detailed exposition of how to plant trees, the writer can simply direct readers to your web site, saying: "check this blog to see how to plan a tree in 5 easy steps". This is instant traffic that you can get just for writing something that can be referenced by others.

Some bloggers are very strong in creating reference articles like this. If you want to increase the visits to your blog quickly you should start to think about how to create reference posts, that can quickly attract repeated visits.

One easy way to do this is to look at the current issues of the area you talk about in your blog. What are the facts that people are interested about? Can you show people how to accomplish this in an easy way?

Even if you don't know how to do something, you can still create lists of useful things that your readers should be aware of. For example, a list of the "top ten stocks for the new year". Or you can write a list of the "twenty worst movies of the decade". This is subjective information, but is also much appreciated by most readers. It can serve as an opinion in which they will base their own conclusions.

GIVING A SINCERE OPINION

Readers are constantly looking for validation for their points of view. Although it might seem that people are just looking for information, most of the time what they really want is to clarify an idea, or to justify something that they are doing (or not doing).

Your posts can serve as a validation for readers. Therefore, just giving an opinion in a subject (preferably a polemic subject) can be of great importance for your readers.

Don't be afraid to give your sincere opinion on topics, especially when that opinion is based on your personal experience or in your understanding of a subject.

For example, during a recent period of high gas prices, a blog author posts regularly about the price of gas on some neighborhood of the city he lived.

Not only that was a great service for readers, but it also increased the audience of his blog. Now, when someone was wondering what the price of gasoline would be in some area of the city, his blog was the first place he or she looked.

It is truly interesting how individuals can do a lot for their communities by just creating a communication channel through their blog. Even during calamities and natural disasters, the power of web publishing has been able to make positive changes.

For example, during the Katrina disaster, a lot of help was offered by bloggers that talked about how the situation of the people in New Orleans was deteriorating. It would be difficult to cite a clearer example of how publishing the information you have locally can make a change for the whole community.

This is a world in which the power that was once in the hands of journalists and other media people can be shared by many. As a blogger, you have not only the possibility but also the power to make a difference in the world.

Posts created with this kind of mentality can catapult your blog to the forefront of an important issue. As a result, you can reap not only the rewards of being recognized for doing a good job, but also the financial returns, such as increased number of advertisements and a space to sell your product, among other opportunities.

AN INTRODUCTION TO AFFILIATE MARKET

Affiliate marketing is one of the most popular methods that new entrepreneurs use to generate a full-time income online. This is partially due to the fact that by being an affiliate marketer you are not required to develop your own product and, in many cases, a website is not required as well. In this information-packed book, you will discover the several methods that successful information marketers use to generate millions of dollars for themselves and their clients, while working from anywhere in the world and having lots of fun.

So, what is affiliate marketing and how can you join the ranks of those who are making money every single day in this exciting market?

A QUICK SUMMARY OF HOW AFFILIATE MARKETING WORKS

Affiliate marketing happens when a product or service is sold by a third party, rather than the developer him or herself.

By selling these products on behalf or in conjunction with the merchant's efforts, the affiliate marketer earns a set commission. Sometimes this payment is given in the form of a flat rate, (example: $10.00 per sale) and other times it's offered through a percentage.

Affiliates can generate revenue by advertising on blogs, websites, directories, and classifieds or by building a list and sending out targeted email campaigns.

Affiliate marketers can also promote third party products via social groups and community networks such as Twitter, Facebook or through information-based community programs like Yahoo Answers, or Hub Pages.

Within each advertisement or article that is developed by an affiliate, there is a special link, unique to that specific affiliate. Whenever their link is clicked on, the merchants website tracks the visit and if a sale results from this activity, the commission is credited to the affiliates account.

AFFILIATE NETWORKS

An affiliate network is a specific program that gives you the ability to be affiliate for many products. Affiliate networks are websites that can handle all transactions including payments, configuration of the affiliate link and support issues are called.

These affiliate networks, such as ClickBank or Commission Junction, process payments, release paychecks to affiliates and work as a go-between for merchants and potential advertising partners.

In the case of ClickBank, an affiliate simply creates one account and can gain access to a wide marketplace of products and services. Within seconds, they can generate unique affiliate links for each and every product that they intend on promoting.

On merchant websites who run their own in-house affiliate programs, affiliate marketers will create individual accounts for each company, who will provide all promotional media including banners, advertisements, pre-written blog posts, forum signatures, classified ad material and even press release documentation or specific keywords to target visitors through advertising circuits like Google Adsense or AdBrite.

Depending on the affiliate network, commissions will vary and it's important to always pay attention to the total amount you will receive per product sale, prior to setting up campaigns or putting in the effort to advertise.

Another thing you want to be careful of is joining an affiliate program who has been established, is reputable and well known. This is necessary because you need to make sure that you will be paid for your promotion efforts. A well stablished affiliate network will send you checks or deposits regularly and make sure that you receive your share of payments.

One problem that affiliate marketers experience from time to time is nonpayment from merchants whose products they have spent time promoting. Joining a well-known affiliate network will make sure that you receive a payment.

If you are new to affiliate marketing, it's often suggested that it's less risky to go with a complete network such as ClickBank, rather than through an independent affiliate program managed by the product developer. (unless of course you are familiar or have a working relationship with these providers).

To help you get familiar with the popular affiliate networks currently available online, here is a quick overview of a handful of the ones most widely used:

CLICKBANK

By far, one of the more popular affiliate communities online. ClickBank offers free affiliate accounts and generating your affiliate link is as simple as clicking a button. Be sure to browse their marketplace daily for current products, updates and hot sellers.

http://www.ClickBank.com

Note: Is it only free to join as an affiliate. If you wish to join as a merchant you will require approval and remittance of a $50 one-time payment.

COMMISSION JUNCTION

Otherwise known as "CJ.com", Commission Junction has been around for many years and is known to pay on time and provide unbeatable support. They also feature hundreds of merchants across the board and regardless of the niche market or subject you are interested in promoting, they are bound to have a few lucrative choices from within their directory.

Commission Junction works a bit differently than Clickbank does in terms of allowing their merchants to manually approve or select affiliates.

With ClickBank, you can choose what products to promote and instantly generate your affiliate link without the requirement of the merchant needing to review your website or approve your registration.

Commission Junction enables their merchants to selectively choose who is allowed to participate in each affiliate program, so if you are new to affiliate marketing, you may end up a bit frustrated when you are turned down due to your website not receiving enough traffic or being focused on specific topics.

http://www.CommissionJunction.com

PAY DOT COM

PayDotCom was created by Mike Filsaime and is similar to ClickBank in terms of product marketplace and niche coverage. One pro to using Pay Dot Com in comparison to ClickBank is that rather than wait every two weeks for a paycheck to be released via postal mail, as ClickBank.com offers, with PayDotCom.com you can receive daily affiliate commission payments directly into your Paypal account. At this time only those who are able to create a Paypal account are able to participate as either a merchant or affiliate within this affiliate marketplace.

SHARE A SALE

ShareASale.com started quite a few years ago, and back then there were few merchants using their services which made it a difficult job for an affiliate to choose high quality products, since there were so few available.

These days, ShareASale.com has grown into an extensive affiliate marketplace, and since all merchants are required to retain a cash balance of funds used to pay affiliates, it's a risk-free way to ensure that you are paid for all of your efforts.

ShareASale, like ClickBank and PayDotCom handle all payments on behalf of the merchants and while ShareASale enables merchants to manually approve affiliates like CJ.com does, from my own personal experience approval has been very quick and in most cases not required at all.

http://www.ShareASale.com

LINK SHARE

Link Share is an ever-growing affiliate marketplace and with it comes a great variety of lucrative and high paying affiliate opportunities.

You can create your Link Share account at http://www.Link-Share.com

USING CPA NETWORKS

CPA, which stands for "Cost Per Action" is a great way to generate extra money as an affiliate marketer, since many new marketers find it easier to generate a lead or a click, than to encourage visitors to become a paid customer. These CPA programs often offer payments on a flat rate basis or a percentage platform.

Apart from being paid per sale, these are networks available online that are willing to pay you for generating other actions from potential customers, on their behalf. Some of these "actions" on CPA networks include:

Paid Per Lead

Generally pays when a visitor gives information such as Names, Email addresses and location. Can also include targeted demographic details.

Paid Per Click

These programs pay you for every click to specific landing or squeeze pages designed by the merchant.

Paid Per Sign Up

These programs pay you for every sign up, typically an offer (free or trial) or for auto responder subscriptions that are confirmed and unique (for list building and email marketing).

Pay Per Download

Software developers will often pay you to generate trial downloads or demo copies of their software with the hope that the user will upgrade to a paid version after the time has run out.

There are quite a few CPA networks that provide you with the ability to register an account and browse the available merchants. Like other affiliate networks, these CPA networks act as a middleman, between you and the merchant.

Here are a few of the most popular CPA networks online:

EPICADVERTISING

EpicAdvertising (previously known as AzoogleAds) is one of the more popular CPA networks, and is consistently growing in size each day. Having been established in 2000, it's known to be one of the more reliable networks, offering payouts per lead, per sale and per download. They have a consolidated payment via check for a minimum of $50.00, with stats and data appearing in real time on their website.

http://www.AzoogleAds.com

MAXBOUNTY

Simple registration process and guaranteed acceptance makes Max Bounty a popular program within communities and online forums based around CPA networking.

Another company that has been active for quite some time and has proven themselves reliable with support and payout.

You can set your payment minimum to a different amount ranging from their minimum of $50, up to 200.00 with payments disbursed monthly via check, bank transfer or Paypal.

International members are also permitted to join with special promotions and campaigns available targeting those groups.

http://www.MaxBounty.com

NEVER BLUE ADS

This network offers a large variety of different campaigns, with a focus on pay per lead programs. With over 20 categories chalk full of viable and lucrative offers, there is no shortage of programs to promote.

Payout is monthly with a minimum requirement of only $25.00, another great reason to join Never Blue Ads.

Initially, on the registration form the only form of payment appears to be via check, however once you are a member you can contact your affiliate representative for additional options including Paypal.

Registration is a simple online registration, and approval is quick, with confirmation within two business days.

http://www.NeverBlueAds.com

Offers Quest - This is a smaller network but is growing in popularity with their focus primarily on Cost Per Lead campaigns. However before you are able to join you must have a fully functional website that is already generating a bit of traffic, written in English (only).

You are also not permitted to offer incentives to your visitors (for action). Payouts are monthly via Paypal or check with a minimum balance requirement of $20.00 for those within the United States or Canada, with a minimum payment requirement of $50.00 for other countries.

http://www.OffersQuest.com

Copeac - This network offers a variety of action based programs including: Cost Per Sale, Cost Per Click, Cost Per Acquisition, and Cost Per Lead, with many categories available and a referral program offering an additional 2% for new advertiser sign ups.

Payment is made via bank wire or check, monthly, with a minimum requirement of $100.00. They also offer a 24 hour emergency hotline if you need help at any time.

During registration, you will be required to verify your location using their automated telephone verification system (similar to the system that Paypal uses)

http://www.Copeac.com

ROCKET PROFIT

This is one of my favorite networks, due to their extremely wide scope in terms of unique Cost Per Lead and Cost Per Sale offers. Payment is available via bank wire, Paypal and check with a minimum requirement of only $25.00 and is disbursed every two weeks.

Applications are reviewed daily, with notification of acceptance received within 2-3 business days.

http://www.RocketProfit.com

HYDRA NETWORK

This is a widely popular CPA network featuring Cost per Click, Cost Per Lead and Cost Per Sale offers. Hydra offers a large assortment of promotional media as well, including email campaigns, co-registration and search.

They also provide very detailed statistics and reporting making it easy for you to monitor your progress in real-time with pre-screening of campaign matches available to ensure that you choose the best campaigns to match your existing audience/traffic.

Payments are every 15 days via bank deposit (wire), and Paypal. Hydra Network also offers the highest payouts for their campaigns.

http://www.HydraNetwork.com

MODERN CLICK

This program is very difficult to get into, as they manually approve every applicant, however once you are accepted you will find quite a few lucrative campaigns to work with including access to advanced tracking tools and real-time stats.

The minimum payment requirement is $25 and the pay period is once a month via check or PayPal.

Their registration process is a bit tedious and lengthy but approval is quick.

http://www.ModernClick.com

DIRECT LEADS

Features a solid program with a wide scope of available offers.

http://www.DirectLeads.com

WEB SPONSORS

This is one of the larger affiliate networks. Their featured offers are lucrative and high quality products that make promoting very easy.

http://www.WebSponsors.com

There are dozens of other CPA networks online with new ones springing up daily. Some of these companies will offer you the ability to feature coupon codes on your website, which prompt visitors to check for new savings frequently boosting traffic to your website and providing a useful service for potential customers.

Others will offer direct content, pre-written ad copy and the more savvy ones will offer you the ability to generate revenue from 404 error pages by splashing their pre-made squeeze page graphics throughout areas of your website not regularly used. It's an extra way of generating additional revenue with absolutely no effort on your part.

GETTING RICH ON CLICKBANK

Clickbank is the largest affiliate network for people willing to promote information products. Since Clickbank is one of the largest and more popular affiliate marketplaces, not to mention how easy it is to get started as an affiliate with them, let's take a closer look at the program and help you get set up so you too can begin to earn daily revenue from their offers.

To begin, visit http://www.ClickBank.com and load their main page. Once there, click on the "Sign Up" link the top nav bar to get started.

The Clickbank sign up page will require a bit of information about you, and one thing you pay particular attention to is the name and address associated with your new account as these can only be changed by writing to a Clickbank representative and requesting modifications.

The address that you supply within the sign-up page is where your affiliate checks will be sent to, so double check this information and be sure that it's accurate.

Fill out the form entirely, choosing a short and memorable account NickName. This nickname, or account ID will be attached to your affiliate link, so you want to be careful to choose something generic if you plan to market different products in a variety of niche marketplaces.

For example, if you are planning to promote products in the "make money niche" and the "Dog Training" niche, you might want not want to choose an account name that is too specific. You should also avoid words like 'sell, promote', etc as those who click on your links will see the keywords you have chosen to use in your ID.

Furthermore, Clickbank limits your account Nickname to only 10 characters or less, so choose something simple and let's move on!

After completing your account registration details, ClickBank will automatically generate a password for you.

You used to be able to choose your own but for the last couple of years, they have their system set up to assign a unique one for each affiliate.

These passwords are often difficult to remember, which increases security. Just be sure to write down your ClickBank username and password because ClickBank does not automatically send the password to you via email when you register.

After you have set up your Clickbank account, your affiliate link will look something like this:

http://Your-ID.publisher.hop.clickbank.net

Don't worry about the link containing ClickBank.net rather than ClickBank.com, this website is still owned and managed by

Clickbank and all of your referral commissions will be correctly applied to your account.

The "publisher" within your links will change depending on the product you promote. To show you exactly what I mean, click on the "Marketplace" link at the very top of the ClickBank website page to view the many different products that you can choose from.

http://www.ClickBank.com/marketplace.htm

Here is where the fun begins. The Clickbank marketplace features products and services within categories and sub-categories, which makes it easy for you to selectively choose to browse only specific topics or niche market material. This can save you a lot of time if you are looking to find new products that are focused on specific topics.

To start, in the "Category" box, select any category you wish. You can also type in specific keywords or choose a sub-category to zone in on your search results.

After you have set up your search query, click on "Go" to load the results window.

In my example below, I have chosen to search through the "Health & Fitness" category, and "Beauty" sub category, with no keywords entered, sorting by Popularity.

From the results window you will see a description of each available product along with a line of green text that includes things like $/sale:, Future $: Total $ /sale etc.

Let me explain what each of these elements mean:

$/sale: The amount of money you earn for each sale.

Future $: Average rebill revenue.

Total $/sale: Average total $ per sale, including all rebills.

%/sale: The percentage of the product sale price that the sale represents.

%/refd: Fraction of publisher's total sales that are referred by affiliates.

grav: The measure of how many affiliates are promoting the product.

For each affiliate paid in the last 8 weeks Clickbank adds an amount between 0.1 and 1.0 to the total. The more recent the last referral, the higher the value added.

The Gravity indicator will tell you how well a product is selling. So a gravity score of 100 means a product is potentially selling better than one with a gravity score of 20.

Looking at your search results, you can easily choose a product that you wish to promote. In order to generate your unique affiliate link, you could click on the link titled "Generate Hoplink".

When you click on "create hoplink" a window will pop up that asks you to enter in your ClickBank username. This is the ID that you chose earlier when you registered for an account.

Just enter in your ClickBank Nickname and click "Create" to generate a unique Clickbank affiliate link!

Note: You can also track your affiliate campaigns by entering in a unique tracking ID (something you will identify or remember). Here is an explanation of the Tracking ID and how it works, according to ClickBanks website:

As an affiliate, the tracking code enhancement provides the power to track and manage your campaigns by tying a specific sale back to the promotion that initiated it.

The tracking code is implemented throughout the ClickBank system as "tid". The format of the hoplink URL with a tracking code is located below.

http://AFFILIATE.PUBLISHER.hop.clickbank.net/?tid=ZZZZZ

In order for the feature to work properly, you must adhere to these standards during its implementation. The tracking code value, which is "zzzzz" in the example above, can be 8 characters long, containing alpha and numeric characters only.

Any value longer than 8 characters will be truncated. Any value containing characters other than alpha or numeric values will have the entire tracking code value removed from the hoplink and order process and, will not show in the transaction report. Tracking code values received lower case characters will be set to all uppercase. The tracking code parameter, which is "tid" in the example above, must be lower case.

You can also view the merchant's sales page by clicking on "view pitch page".

CHOOSING PRODUCTS TO PROMOTE

In order to make the most money from your marketing efforts, you need to learn how to easily choose surefire sellers, products that are hot, in demand and essentially easy to sell.

Thankfully, there are a few different resources available that will help both new and seasoned affiliate marketers select winning products from along the hundreds featured within the marketplace.

Two of these resources include:

CB Engine, available at http://www.cbengine.com

CB Trends, available at http://www.CBTrends.com

Let's take a closer look at these two resources and learn exactly how they can instantly help you choose the best products based on your market.

CB Trends offers information regarding product performance, which includes the history of specific products within the marketplace.

All you need to do is enter in the vendors ID (which you can find from within the ClickBank marketplace), and the CB Trends search engine will load relevant data associated with that product. This information can include popularity breakdown, gravity, and earnings per sale, percent per dale, referrals and commission earnings that show over a period of time.

By browsing the different graphs that will appear after each search, you are able to easily analyze the different aspects of each product including overall popularity, how well the product has done in the past, how many affiliates are promoting the product and more.

While dissecting this data isn't always the easiest thing to do if you are a new affiliate marketer, as you continue to promote products and detect which ones are doing better in terms of conversion, you will begin to better understand the information available on sites like CBTrends and use it to your advantage in creating better, higher converting campaigns.

CB Engine also offers a free search utility, very much the same as CB Trends. However, CB Engine requires a membership ($39.95 one time fee for a years access to graphics, stats and history tracking).

If you would like to preview the members area, CB Engine provides a free 15 day trial, available on their website.

TOOLS OF THE TRADE

In order to be the best affiliate marketer that you can, you will need to learn how to properly manage your campaigns, stay focused and organized and always design a strategy before you begin to promote each product.

AUTORESPONDERS

An autoresponder is an essential part of the toolbox for every web marketer. It serves a lot of purposes when helping you keep in contact with your customers.

For instance, while a website or blog isn't required to work as an affiliate, it certainly makes the job easier in terms of having a landing page to send visitors to, and in order to direct them to multiple affiliate products you tend to promote. You could also use this blog or website as a way of generating leads through an autoresponder service such as www.GetResponse.com or www.Aweber.com

By creating a mailing list of people interested in specific products or services, you can easily send out an advertisement containing your affiliate link whenever you want to. This will cut your work down by over half, and increase your profits dramatically.

An autoresponder account costs between $15 - $25 a month but is a worthwhile investment. I spent years manually promoting products before I ever decided to take advantage of the power that a mailing list provides and when I finally got started generating leads and creating targeted lists, I was able to easily triple my income literally overnight.

USING WORDPRESS

Designing a website isn't always the easiest thing to do, especially if you are not familiar with CSS or HTML. Outsourcing these projects can be costly and even a bit overwhelming if you haven't done it before. Thankfully, there is an easy solution to this problem.

It's called WordPress, and unless you have been living under a heavy rock for the last couple of years, it's likely you have heard about it.

WordPress is a blog platform, a free script that lets people like us quickly (and near effortlessly) set up a website in seconds. You simply download the Wordpress package, upload it to your host, and install it from any web browser.

The great thing about Wordpress is that not only is it entirely free, but with so many people using it, the tools and resources available to enhance or customize it, are endless.

You can easily find the perfect theme for your blog regardless of what niche market you are focused on within the hundreds of free theme directories online. You simply upload the theme into your Wordpress admin area, and you're good to go.

Rather than provide a detailed Wordpress guide, I will direct you to explore Wordpress by visiting their website at http://www.WordPress.org

You can find their five minute quick installation guide (which makes installing a complete no-brainer) and when you are ready to customize your website, you can browse through the popular free directories such as:

http://themes.Wordpress.net

http://www.FreeWPThemes.net

http://www.SkinPress.com

http://www.ThemeLab.com

Of course, Wordpress also features free themes on their own website as well, that showcases contributions from WP designers:

http://Wordpress.org/extend/themes

In order to host a WordPress blog, you will need an affordable hosting account. I personally recommend using www.HostGator.com as they are easy to use, affordable and will set up your account within a couple of hours.

You should be sure to check for a recent coupon and save yourself a few bucks by visiting my favorite coupon directory site, www.RetailMeNot.com

(You can find there a coupon that will give you one month of hosting at Hostgator absolutely free!)

As for a domain name, once again you want something similar to your ClickBank username in terms of being generic. Unless you plan to promote only one type of product on your website, you will need a domain name that could easily be used for multiple niche markets.

Take your time and be sure to choose something memorable. I use www.NameCheap.com and www.GoDaddy.com for my domain name registrations, however www.Moniker.com is another great resource.

Once again, be sure to check the RetailMeNot.com coupon directory to find additional rebates on domain names. You can usually get at least $2.00 off a domain name just for applying a current coupon to your order.

Remember: every dollar counts!

TRAFFIC GENERATION 101

So, you have a brandable domain name that is easy to remember, you have a ClickBank account and by now, you should have a website, either as a WordPress blog or a full out site (if you are skilled ;)

So, what's the next step in our journey to affiliate marketing success?

Traffic!

Without traffic, our website is flat, dead in the water, pointless. So, how do we generate traffic to our website affordably, or better yet FREE?

There are many ways to send an instant rush of traffic to your website at no cost. These methods often referred to as "bum marketing" take a bit of work, but they are surefire tactics that yield incredible results if done correctly.

The first method is through SEO, Search Engine Optimization.

SEO means that you will optimize your site in a way that your prospects will find it easily when searching on Google or other search engines. Therefore, you will be optimizing the site for search engines.

The problem with relying on SEO is that is certainly isn't a quick way of harnessing traffic. In fact, optimizing your website or blog can take days, even weeks to actually begin ranking, let alone ranking well, for specific keywords. Worse: depending on the competition, it can take an awful lot of work to boost up your ranking, if achievable at all.

In addition to the time it takes to rank well at times, you also have to deal with the overload of Google advertisers, those guys who appear in the right hand column on your search results page (see below). These advertisers pay for every click on their ads, and unless you have the funds to create your own campaigns, they can often be extremely costly.

However, that doesn't mean that we will disregard SEO altogether, in fact, every good affiliate marketer should know the basics to SEO and apply these techniques to their blogs and websites.

So, let's take a closer look at how you can optimize your website and rank in the daddy of all search engines: Google

To start, the most important aspects of ranking in Google is how well you target your keywords. You want to make sure that you are using the very best keyword that you can, and one that is relevant to your website or the products that you plan to promote.

These keywords will be placed within your websites title tags, so if you were promoting a product called "Overnight Wealth", you would want to include "Overnight Wealth" in the title tag of the page that provides information about this product (and course, features your affiliate link).

One of the best ways to generate affiliate commissions is through review or rating based websites and we'll cover that in more detail later on, but just as an example, if I were reviewing a product called "Dog Training Secrets", the keywords I would include within the title tag of that landing page would be "Dog Training Secrets". Not "Dog Secrets", not "Training Secrets', but the full product name, "Dog Training Secrets", spaced in individual keywords just like the product name would be on the front cover of a book.

You add your title into the source of your page or if you are using Wordpress, you simply log into your admin panel and change the name of your blog to one that is based on specific keywords. Wordpress will automatically update every page and post with this keyword title.

The title tag however isn't the only aspect of on-site SEO. There are other elements, equally as important including:

Page Title
Be sure to place your keyword within the Page Title itself.

Page Headings
The first line or two on your website is your page heading, usually larger than your body text and is the first thing visitors see to your website. While you want your page heading to captivate them and prompt them to read further, you also want to ensure that your keywords are included within your page heading.

Top, Middle and Bottom of your page.
You really want to sprinkle your keywords throughout your

content or article. Don't over-saturate (keyword stuff) your content because it will sound funny and probably not make much sense to the average reader, but definitely pay attention to how you are crafting your article and do your best to weave your keywords throughout your copy so it sounds natural.

If you want to be certain of your keyword density, you can use the free tool available at http://www.live-keyword-analysis.com to evaluate your copy. Just copy and paste your text into the box, enter up to three keywords and the script will detect the keyword density of your document, instantly.

It's a rule of thumb to ensure that your keyword density never rises above 5%, otherwise search engines like Google.com may penalize you for keyword stuffing.

Of course, another aspect of writing good keyword-based article content that the search engine will eat up like candy is ensuring that your content is fresh, relevant and unique. Whether you re-write an existing article out there, purchase private label right content or hire a freelance writer, you want to make absolutely certain that your content is as unique as possible.

If you do go with pre-written content, be sure to change the information by at least 40%, preferably 60% or more if you can. It really doesn't take much effort to re-write existing information and even if you are unsure about the topic or know little about the subject, just spent an hour conducting online research by browsing existing websites, article directories and blogs to compile the information you need. Then, start from scratch and re-write the entire article. It's something many affiliate marketers and even mainstream article marketers do to produce fresh content and fresh ideas.

One last thing to cover regarding on-site SEO is using anchor-based text links. These are links that show specific keywords rather than a URL to a site.

For example, a regular link might look like this:

http://www.AffiliateShortcut.com

Whereas a keyword anchor text link would look like this

Discover Affiliate Shortcuts

Be sure to use anchor-based links whenever possible, both within your copy and content and when linking to your site on directories, classifieds or other blogs.

THE PROS AND CONS OF OWNING AN ONLINE BUSINESS

Working from your house has numerous advantages, but also comes with its disadvantages. Building a successful online business is a dream come true for many people around the world, though to some, it is not always fun and games. Sources have it that you can survive on online businesses and enjoy the freedom of earning real money from your passions. As earlier mentioned, running an online business is not always a walk in the park, and therefore it is wise not to underestimate the hard work that a successful online business requires.

To understand what it entails to run an online business, let us take a look at the pros and cons of running online businesses.

PROS OF RUNNING AN ONLINE BUSINESS

1) Flexible schedule and rules.

Owning an online job allows you to create your rules and be your boss. With the flexibility that comes with self-employment, one can even create time to see friends and family.

2) Low startup costs.

One key benefit of owning an online business is the low starting cost. Sources have it that you can start a website with less than $100, and as your business grows, you can invest more in it. An online business gives you the liberty of working from your house, and requires no leasing costs. You do not have to worry about employees salary too!

3) You become the boss.

Running your own online business gives you the mandate of setting the rules and regulations. Nobody tells you what to do, and you get an opportunity of controlling your destiny. You get to make decisions about marketing, product or service development, customer service, and pretty much everything related to your business.

.

THE CONS OF RUNNING AN ONLINE BUSINESS

1) Long working hours

For any business to succeed, it calls for hard work and long working hours. Starting an online job from scratch takes a good amount of time to be successful and in some cases, people are required to work on weekends to reach their targets.

2) Requires a lot of discipline.

With all the freedom that comes with running your own business, discipline is fundamental. Time one takes for breaks should be limited, and more focus should be made to reach the set target.

Running an online business has its pros and cons. Low startup cost, and setting your rules are some of the advantages of starting an online business. Additionally, for all the people who are not afraid of working for long hours, online business is meant for you.

THINGS YOU SHOULD KNOW BEFORE STARTING AN INTERNET BUSINESS

Starting an internet business can be a lot of fun. Unfortunately, if you jump right in without doing a little research first, you could find yourself becoming overwhelmed very quickly. Some people make it look easy. The truth of the matter is that the people who make it look easy are people who did a lot of research beforehand. They understood what they were assuming to such a significant degree, they were able to avoid some of the common pitfalls of starting an Internet business.

To be sure, you can avoid those pitfalls, as well.

BEFORE YOU START AN INTERNET BUSINESS

The great thing about the concept of an internet business is the fact that you are referring to a very, very wide spectrum of possibility. The business can be as large or as small as you want/need it to be. Here are a few things that any internet business entrepreneur should keep in mind, before they do something like run out and buy a domain:

- Have a plan: While you don't need to have a detailed, formal business plan, you still need to come up with some mode of attack. This can include researching potential competitors, developing a sense of what you want to market to which group of people.

- Establish a budget, and keep something else in mind: Your business is going to need a budget, regardless of its size. When budgeting an internet business, there are two things to keep in mind. First, remember that your budget needs to be realistic. Secondly, you want to appreciate the fact that in all likelihood, youre going to lose money before you make money.

- Customers will want to meet you: Standing out from the pack with an internet business can be really challenging. Sometimes, it gets awfully close to impossible. With that in mind, remember that one good way of establishing a unique brand is to filter your own personality into everything that defines your internet business. People are going to want to know who they are buying goods and services from. Don't reveal more than you are comfortable with, but understand that you will have to create a public identity for customer service purposes and more.

- Do something you're actually going to enjoy: Large or small, an internet business can be a lot of work. Make sure you are doing something you will be able to enjoy, which comes in handy when things take a turn for the challenging.

TOP 5 MISTAKES ONLINE BUSINESS OWNERS MAKE

Every business owner makes mistakes. Even the likes of Warren Buffett, Richard Marx and Elon Musk have made mistakes in their businesses. The quintessential need is not be perfect and averting every mistake but to avoid those ones that will cost your business dearly. Here are top five mistakes online business owners make.

Cheap Infrastructure

A business must always remain sustainable and for that it is necessary to remain reasonable with all expenses or recurring financial liabilities. However, affordability should not compel a business owner to make decisions that will not augur well for the enterprise. For instance, opting for cheap hosting plans will save you money but the real cost has to be assessed. Hosting plans that cost very little every month will have severely capped bandwidth, there will be hardly any worthwhile security for the website, the online presence will be compromised as the uptime will not be a hundred percent or even close and any kind of scaling will be dealt with very slowly. Infrastructure is the backbone of any industry or business. Online business owners often opt for cheap infrastructure.

Outsourcing Everything

Globalization has ushered in an era when you can find people to do everything at a fraction of a cost than what you would have paid in the pre-globalization days. It is not fair to state that the quality of professionals or their skills has waned but it is true that outsourcing has its pitfalls. You can and should outsource anything that you are not very good at. From website designing to accounting, you can and must hire experts. Also, note that out-sourcing is not necessarily off-shoring. You can hire contractors or companies based in your city, state or country. The trouble lies in outsourcing everything. When online business owners don't have complete control on any of the assets of the company or the day-to-day affairs affecting one or all existential aspects of the enterprise, then the business is bound to suffer sooner or later.

Lack of Diversification

Many business owners are content with their zeroed in focus on one or a few niches. It is perfectly acceptable to focus on one or a few niches but you need to diversify to sustain your overall empire through the years. Every niche goes through upswings and downswings. You can always enjoy the upswings but you need to plan for the downswings.

Cease in Upgrading

Many online business owners launch their enterprises with state of the art propositions and then stop upgrading. It is not just the technological infrastructure that needs to be upgraded but also the quality of products and services, the manner in which the business is managed and how the clients are dealt with.

Ignoring Competition

Digital enterprises can spring up in no time and usurp the market share of a major brand in a brisk few weeks. Ignoring competition is a surefire way to ring the death knell for the business.

TOP REASONS WHY YOU SHOULD START AN ONLINE BUSINESS

Starting an online business is no cakewalk. Anyone who suggests that an online business is easy to run or one can make a million dollars in no time is not being realistic. There are serious challenges in running any type of business, be it offline or online. Yet, it is better to start an online business. Here are the top reasons why you should start an online business.

- There are innumerable people in the world who have great ideas but they are unable to manifest those ideas owing to lack of funds and resources. Starting any type of traditional or conventional business requires substantial investments. Most online businesses can be launched with very little investment. Even a neighborhood convenience store requires a handsome investment and that money is locked in for years. The storeowner doesn't recuperate the entire investment in one year or even five years. You don't need such massive capital to start an online business.

- Most traditional businesses have a significant threshold that must be attended to. You cannot start very small and expect to become a medium sized enterprise or a major brand in a few months. An online business can be launched as a very small initiative and it can grow quickly. This growth doesn't have to be fueled by a fortune in investment or tremendous expansion in sheer real estate. Expansion of online enterprises is much easier and hence a business can become sustainable in a much shorter period of time.

- An online business can be started by anyone, from anywhere and it can make its presence felt anywhere in the world. You don't need to be in a particular state or country to sell your digital products or services. Conventional businesses are bound by location, the immediate target audience and local influence. An online business can start local and become global in a few months.

- The sheer scope of online business opens up a colossal realm of opportunities. Ideas that wouldn't have made much business sense a few years ago are now gold mines that can make one a millionaire, if not a billionaire. There is room for every innovative idea and ever type of business that can add some value to the lives of people or companies around the world.

- An online business allows entrepreneurs to make as much or as little money as one want depending on the time, effort and resources one is willing to invest in the enterprise. There is of course the life work balance and personal freedom, both of which are unmatched perks of running an online business.

TREAT YOUR BUSINESS LIKE A BUSINESS, NOT A HOBBY

A hobby can be turned into a business but a business can never become a hobby. There are some rich and famous people who have the luxury to conduct business while indulging in leisure. For the lesser mortals, business and leisure don't go hand in hand. Any business requires serious investments, be it material such as money and infrastructure or immaterial as time and effort. Here are some of the many reasons why you should treat your business like a business and not a hobby.

- A hobby is more of a pastime in which you have substantial passion. A business can never be a pastime. There are serious consequences. You may lose money. If you have employees, then those jobs are at stake and hence their livelihoods. If you have products or services that people depend on then you are risking that and your consumers or customers will be left high and dry if you fail to deliver. A hobby is absolutely personal. No business is completely personal. A business will have direct and indirect impacts on the lives of many people. A startup can still be treated as a hobby till there is serious money in it and the potential or actual impacts on others. Beyond that point, a business must be treated like a business.

• A hobby has a lot to do with emotion over pragmatism. Most hobbies develop out of sheer love for something. There is little or no aspiration to monetize the skill or whatever you are creating. The purpose is to give form to your feelings or the skills you possess. Essentially, a hobby is about emotions. A business can stem from a particular or cluster of emotions but it can never be managed or run emotionally. You must always have a pragmatic take on your business and that will not happen if you treat it as a hobby or an emotional endeavor.

• A hobby often has to dabble through spells of procrastination. You cannot allow procrastination to seep in when you are running an actual business. There are deadlines in the real world, bottom lines and real money at stake. You cannot take your own sweet time to develop or deliver something. Treating your business like a hobby will be the recipe for disaster and sooner than later your enterprise will cease to exist or be unsustainable. Also, a hobby is principally about personal satisfaction. A business is not.

USING FREE VS PAID MERCHANT ACCOUNTS

For many who own and operate their own internet businesses, the need for a merchant account is a crucial one. Simply put, a merchant account is something that allows you to accept online transactions, which can involve using credit cards or debit cards. It isn't hard to imagine how important something like this can be for an online business.

Also, it shouldn't be hard to imagine the necessity of making sure you have a merchant account that makes sense for your business and your needs. It comes down to choosing between two possibilities, which are free merchant accounts, or paid merchant accounts. Obviously, a new internet business will want to keep costs down, so it makes sense to want a free merchant account. At the same time, a savvy individual would probably tell you that even these days, there is really no such thing as free.

SO WHICH WAY IS THE RIGHT WAY TO GO?

Free Merchant Accounts Or Paid Merchant Accounts

One of the first things to understand with free/paid merchant accounts is that with paid merchant accounts, you are talking about an expense that can strike you as particularly high. This is certainly true when your new internet business needs to adhere to a pretty tight budget. The costs with paid merchant accounts can also vary from one provider to the other.

At the same time, many internet business owners would argue that paid merchant accounts pay for themselves many times over. Strong processing/chargeback rates are common with free accounts. Furthermore, youre not going to get very much in the way of features with free accounts, if you get anything at all. Paid accounts can take advantage of things like customer service, which is certainly something thats nice to have, in the event that you run into some problems with a payment. Technical service can also certainly prove to be a lifesaver. Youre not going to find that with a free merchant account.

However, free can be useful in the early stages. If you don't think you can afford a paid account, then a free option can be a useful temporary solution. However, you are going to need to do some research, and determine how much you are ultimately going to need to pay in fees. Even over a short period of time, these costs can prove to be higher as a whole, than how much you would to spend for a paid merchant account.

WHAT NEXT?

Now that you have a good idea of how to generate traffic, you should start with one of the techniques described in this chapter.

Remember, if you don't do the work, nobody will find your website. The nice thing about the Internet, however, is that you can leverage your work in order to get much more than you imagined.

By applying some of these techniques, you can start with just a few visitors per day. But with time and persistence, these visitors will add up and provide you with great profits.

FINAL WORDS

Thanks for reading this eBook! I hope you now have a much better idea of what we do to make money with blogs. The process is simple, but it takes some initial work, as you learned in the pages of this eBook.

But, above all, I would say that becoming successful in the web requires persistence. The magic of making money in the Internet can only happen if you apply yourself and do the necessary steps. Thousands of people have created a wealthy lifestyle using this process. Now it is your turn!

ADDITIONAL RESOURCES

This eBook was brought to you by moneum.com, a group dedicated to creating the best material in the Internet on web-based and personal businesses.

To put in practice what you learn in this eBook and get even faster results, we recommend that you check out our additional learning material. Here is a quick list of other titles:

☐ Web Magic Profits

This is our most popular package. This eBook tells everything you need to start generating incredible amounts of money in a web-based business. In this eBook you will learn important skills such as:

- Becoming an affiliate seller.
- Generating traffic.
- Creating websites that sell.
- Managing lists.
- And much more…

Product description: 112 pages, PDF format, with an Appendix, $29 (available now).

☐ The Affiliate Solution

Learn how to start a business without creating your own products! Promote some of the large number of the physical or digital products available in the Internet. In this information-packed eBook, your will learn:

- How to start as an affiliate.
- The importance of working in a niche.
- How to drive visitors to your campaigns.
- Using Google and Bing to display targeted ads.
- Using you email list to sell more.
- And much more...

Product description: 88 pages, PDF format, with an Appendix, $29